ABC Keystone Safari Rhymes

**Written By: GaGa
(AKA) Janice Abernethy**

**Artwork and Photography By: GaGa:
(AKA) Janice Abernethy**

Copyrighted Material

Copyright © 2023 Janice Abernethy

Illustrations © 2023 Janice Abernethy

Website: jabernethy.com

ISBN: 979-8-218-31779-9 Paperback

Published by Janice Abernethy

E-mail: abcanimalrhymes@gmail.com

No portion of this book may be reproduced, stored in a retrieval system, or transmitted in any form or by any means, mechanical, electronic, photocopying, recording, or otherwise, without the written permission of the publisher.

Copyrighted Material

The images featured in this book were captured within the captivating surroundings of Keystone Safari Park, situated in Grove City, Pennsylvania. The majority of these photos were taken within the "Walk-Through" area of the zoo, while a few were shot in the Safari Drive-Through section.

Keystone Safari offers an engaging and interactive zoo experience that you won't want to miss. Whether you're young or old, there's something here for everyone to enjoy. This walkthrough zoo allows you to get up close and personal with a variety of animals, giving you the chance to feed and interact with them. Additionally, for the more adventurous visitors, there are zip-line courses available for both older kids and adults, as well as a specially designed zip-line course for younger children.

Just half a mile down the road, you'll find the Safari Drive-Through, a thrilling and engaging attraction. Here, you can get up close and personal with most of the animals either from the comfort of your car window or aboard the repurposed army trucks operated by the park.

**Please be aware that not all the animals featured in this book may be present at Keystone Safari during your visit. Keystone Safari frequently welcomes new additions, including baby animals, and some of its residents may also be shared with its sister zoo, Living Treasures, located in New Castle. Living Treasures is another fantastic zoo worth exploring! I strongly encourage you to consider visiting both zoos. You can conveniently access the websites of Keystone Safari and Living Treasures by scanning the QR codes provided below to discover more about these exceptional wildlife destinations.

About the Author

Janice Abernethy, known as Jan Ford, grew up in Mars, Pennsylvania, surrounded by her parents and five brothers. Her childhood was filled with playful interactions with her brothers, from playing school to engaging in sports like baseball. Jan's love for animals was evident, as she frequently brought home animals and dreamed of living on a ranch one day. She married her dream man, Sam, and together they had two daughters and a son. Despite her affinity for technology, she surprised everyone by pursuing a career in teaching. She worked tirelessly to obtain a degree in elementary and special education while caring for her family. Jan's teaching journey took her to Greenville Area School District, where she blended her passion for animals and nature with education. Her classroom featured various class pets, and she spearheaded a schoolyard habitat project with her students. After 23 fulfilling years in teaching, she retired alongside her husband, Sam. The couple enjoy their retirement on their farm, Abernethy Acres, filled with horses, and embark on RV travels across the country. Their grandson, Ike's birth inspired Jan to write a children's book, which she illustrated after teaching herself art through YouTube tutorials. The book, initially intended as a Christmas gift, was published to share joy with other children.

Jan's retirement projects, class websites, and blogs can be explored on her website, where she showcases her multifaceted talents. To learn more about the author or her teaching journey, visit her website at https://jabernethy.com.

ABC KEYSTONE SAFARI RHYMES

Dedicated to my grandson, Ike, and my granddaughter, Penny. Ike who is a connoisseur of zoos, thinks Keystone Safari is the BEST! He can't wait to share all the animals with his brand new baby sister, Penny.

GaGa

A is for ADDAX

ADDAX

 Mammal

 Herbivore

Critically Endangered

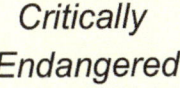

A is for Addax, an antelope that's white,
Spiral horns on my head are a striking sight.

I'm a herbivore, I eat grass, leaves, and seeds.
I don't drink much water, just enough for my needs.

The Sahara Desert is my habitat
That's in Africa. Not sure if you knew that.

What else can I tell you? There is so much more!
Come to Keystone Safari and let's take a tour!

B is for BEAR

B is for Bear. The American Black Bear.
I eat fruits, grasses, fish and I don't like to share.

I go to sleep for months. It's called hibernate.
I wake up feeling refreshed. Isn't that great?

My eyesight and hearing are better than yours.
Climbing trees with my claws is one of my chores.

What else can I tell you? There is so much more!
Come to Keystone Safari and let's take a tour!

NORTH AMERICAN BLACK BEAR

M   Mammal

O   Omnivore

Not Endangered

CAMEL

 Mammal

 Herbivore

Bactrian are Critically Endangered

C is for camel. Different kinds, there are two.
We have one hump or two humps. Come see at the zoo.

Dromedary has one hump just like a D.
Bactrian Camels-two humps, and so does a B.

Some Bactrian still live in the wild. And we're rare.
Dromedary-more common; there is much to compare

What else can I tell you? There is so much more!
Come to Keystone Safari and let's take a tour!

One Hump
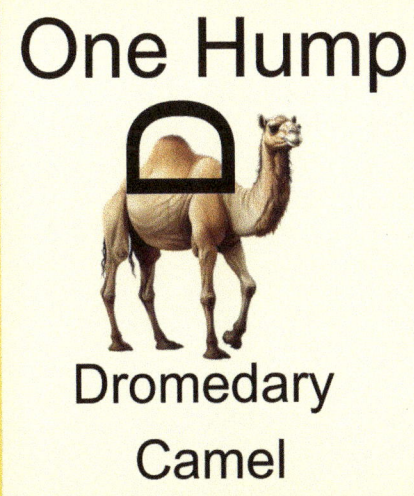
Dromedary Camel

Two Humps
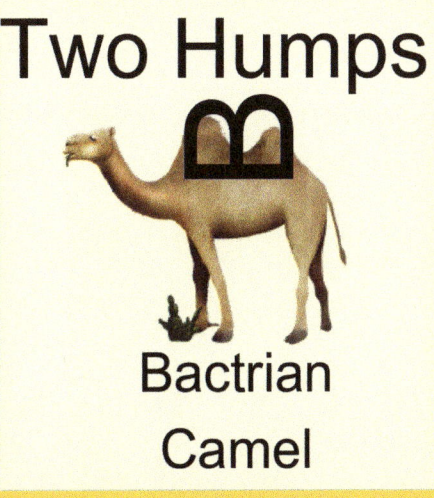
Bactrian Camel

D is for DUCK

DUCKS
(Waterfowl)

B Bird

O Omnivore

Not Endangered

D is for duck. I am the most common bird.
One hundred thirty species, is what I've heard.

I'm born without feathers. I can swim, so don't fret.
I'm a special type of bird that likes to get wet.

When I hatch I'll follow the first person I see!
Forever my friend, that is what you will be!

What else can I tell you? There is so much more!
Come to Keystone Safari and let's take a tour!

E is for EMU

E is for Emu. I'm a super fun bird.
I make people laugh, because I am absurd.

Liberty Mutual commercials is how I'm known
If you've never seen one, look it up on your phone.

Dingoes, eagles, snakes, just some predators of mine.
But my powerful kick keeps me safe just fine.

What else can I tell you? There is so much more!
Come to Keystone Safari and let's take a tour!

F is for FOX

F is for fox, a Bat-Eared Fox in this case.
I have really big ears and a pretty cute face.

Dung beetles and termites are some of my prey.
Chicks, eggs, and lizards, I eat with no delay.

Eating veggies really puts me in a good mood.
I barely need water. I get it from food.

What else can I tell you? There is so much more.
Come to Keystone Safari and let's take a tour!

BAT-EARED FOX

M Mammal

C Carnivore

Not Endangered

G is for GIRAFFE

G is for giraffe. I'm a mammal. I'm tall.
My best friend, the Oxpecker, is a bird that is small.

A secret I'll tell you, we giraffes pick our nose.
With our really long tongue. I mean it. We're pros.

I don't make any sounds or noises for you.
It's not like I can't, it's because I don't want to.

What else can I tell you? There is so much more!
Come to Keystone Safari and let's take a tour!

RETICULATED GIRAFFE

M Mammal

H Herbivore

Endangered

H is for HYENA

H is for hyena. I am fierce and tough.
I eat wildebeasts, zebras, and other stuff.

I can live in a clan with eighty or more.
I eat veggies and meat. I'm an omnivore.

I have a crazy laugh that doesn't mean fun.
My giggles and cackles mean you better run.

What else can I tell you? There is so much more!
Come to Keystone Safari and let's take a tour!

I is for INDIAN RUNNER

INDIAN RUNNER

B Bird

O Omnivore

Not Endangered

I is for Indian Runner. A duck that can't fly.
I can run, but not fly, even if I try.

Some call me Penguin Duck, cause that's how I walk.
I don't waddle, I'm upright just like a corn stalk.

Marshland water fresh or salt, for this duck.
I love all kinds of water and all kinds of muck.

What else can I tell you? There is so much more!
Come to Keystone Safari and let's take a tour!

INDIAN RUNNER

J is for JAPANESE KOI FISH

J is for a fish you call Japanese Koi.
I have such great beauty that you can enjoy.

I was just a plain carp 'til the Japanese got me.
They bred me for color and variety.

The oldest Koi fish is two hundred fifty.
Found by counting rings on scales, just like a tree.

What else can I tell you? There is so much more!
Come to Keystone Safari and let's take a tour!

K is for
KOOKABURRA

K is for Kookaburra. I am a bird.
I can laugh like a human, but I can't say a word.

I'm a carnivore, which means I like to eat meat.
And stealing food from snakes is my very best feat.

I am known for a song. Look it up. You will see.
First line...Kookaburra sits in the old Gum Tree.

What else can I tell you? There is so much more!
Come to Keystone Safari and let's take a tour!

KOOKABURRA

B — Bird

O — Omnivore

Not Endangered

L is for LION

LION

M Mammal

C Carnivore

Not Endangered

L is for Lion. The Barbary type is rare.
Less than a hundred left, I want you to care.

I used to be royal, the pet of a king.
I once lived in Africa. No longer a thing.

In the wild, I'm like dinosaurs completely extinct.
Zookeepers are saving me. That doesn't stink.

What else can I tell you? There is so much more!
Come to Keystone Safari and let's take a tour!

M is for MANDRILL

M is for Mandrill. Some call me a baboon.
But I'm really a monkey and live in Cameroon.

I like to eat berries and insects and more.
I eat fruit. I eat reptiles. I'm an omnivore.

Do you know Rafiki? He's a Mandrill, you know.
Just look at his face on the Lion King show.

What else can I tell you? There is so much more!
Come to Keystone Safari and let's take a tour!

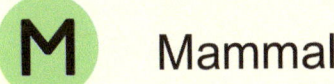

N is for NIGERIAN DWARF GOAT

N is for the cute Nigerian Dwarf Goat.
Brown, black, gray, white combinations, my coat.

Domesticated by man means I am not wild.
I give milk, cheese, or meat. My temperament's mild.

I am loud when I talk and sometimes I shriek.
I am fun and outgoing and not at all meek.

What else can I tell you? There is so much more!
Come to Keystone Safari and let's take a tour.

O is for OSTRICH

OSTRICH

B Bird

O Omnivore

Vulnerable

O is for Ostrich. I'm a really fast bird.
Forty miles per hour. Wow! Isn't that absurd?

Along with zebras, wildebeest and antelope,
Our habitat is grasslands, together we cope.

My eyes are soooo big? Five times bigger than yours!
I can see our predators coming. It's one of my chores.

What else can I tell you? There is so much more!
Come to Keystone Safari and let's take a tour!

P is for PENGUIN

PENGUIN

B Bird

C Carnivore

Endangered

P is for Penguin, a bird that cannot fly
I'm an African Penguin. I'm different. Here's why.

Most penguins live where it's cold, but I like it warm.
A warm coastal climate in Africa's my norm.

I can drink salt water thanks to a salt gland.
I can bray like a donkey. Isn't that grand?

What else can I tell you? There is so much more!
Come to Keystone Safari and let's take a tour!

Q is for
QUIRKY, GIANT ANTEATER

GIANT ANTEATER

M Mammal

I Insectivore

Vulnerable

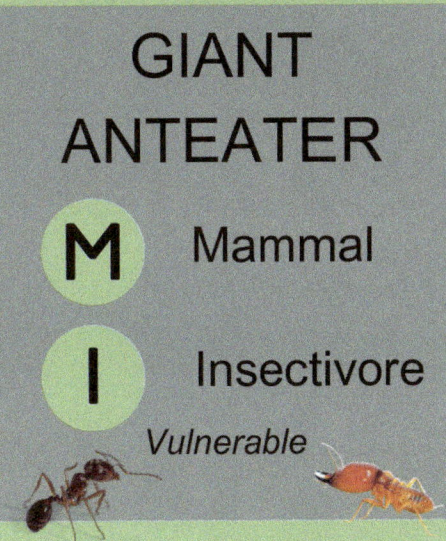

Quirky Giant Anteater begins with Q.
Quirky means I'm odd, I think that's good, don't you?

I can eat 30 thousand insects in one day.
Mostly ants and termites, but even bees are prey.

My tongue is two feet long, No teeth, but that's okay.
My snout works like a vacuum. No insect gets away!

What else can I tell you? There is so much more!
Come to Keystone Safari and let's take a tour.

R is for REINDEER

R is for Reindeer. Some call us Caribou.
The males have antlers and the females do too.

I am a ruminant. Cloven hooves are my feet,
I have four stomachs, and I do not eat meat.

I can live in the tundra. I am built for it.
My hollow hair traps heat and I have heaps of grit.

What else can I tell you? There is so much more!
Come to Keystone Safari and let's take a tour!

REINDEER

M Mammal

H Herbivore

Vulnerable

S is for SAFARI

S is for Safari. Keystone is the best.
Focused on conserving puts this zoo above the rest.

Endangered species in the wild with their numbers low,
Are given second chances here to thrive and grow.

Take the Keystone truck or drive your car and you'll view,
Wildebeest, Rhea, Yak, Bison, even Emu.

What else can I tell you? There is so much more!
Come to Keystone Safari and let's take a tour!

T is for TORTOISE

TORTOISE

R Reptile

H Herbivore

*Endangered
(Sulcata Tortoises)*

Aldabra Tortoise

T is for Tortoise, a terrestrial being.
Some call us turtles and I'm not disagreeing.

All tortoises are turtles. Are turtles the same?
No. Turtles who like water have a different name.

I don't like water and I live much longer.
I'm a herbivore and my shell is stronger.

What else can I tell you? There is so much more!
Come to Keystone Safari and let's take a tour!

Leopard Tortoise

THURMAN
(My Sulcata Tortoise)
Ike and Thurman
(GaGa's Sulcata Tortoise)

U is for UNCAGED GUINEA PIGS

GUINEA PIG

M Mammal

H Herbivore

Not Endangered

U is for the lucky Uncaged Guinea Pig.
At Keystone my setup is really quite big.

I'm a herbivore, meaning I eat grass and hay
I am active and awake twenty hours a day.

I'm a rodent, not a pig. I'm more like a rat.
And I'm not from Guinea. How do you like that?

What else can I tell you? There is so much more!
Come to Keystone Safari and let's take a tour!

V is for VALAIS SHEEP

VALAIS BLACK-NOSED SHEEP

M Mammal

H Herbivore
Threatened

V is for Valais Black-Nosed Sheep. I'm black and white.
And if you heard I am the cutest sheep, that's right.

I have special markings like black on my knees
I'm a herbivore. I eat grass, and leaves from trees.

I'm social and friendly, I'm not shy at all..
If you give me a name, I will come when you call.

What else can I tell you? There is so much more!
Come to Keystone Safari and let's take a tour!

W is for
WHITE-NAPED CRANE

W is for the elegant White-Naped Crane.
I have pinkish legs, I eat insects, meat, and grain.

My mom laid an egg, but both parents built the nest.
They work as a team to see that I get the best.

I dance when I'm happy. I dance when I'm sad.
I dance to find partners. Now isn't that rad?

What else can I tell you? There is so much more!
Come to Keystone Safari and let's take a tour!

WHITE NAPED CRANE

B Bird

O Omnivore

Vulnerable

X is for the almost EXTINCT LEMUR

X is for the lemur, eXtinct are some types.
Endangered are the lemurs that have tails with stripes.

I'm a Ring-Tailed Lemur. It's not safe to be free.
All lemurs are from Madagascar, even me.

Habitat destruction is the cause of our plight.
We are counting on humans to make it alright.

What else can I tell you? There is so much more!
Come to Keystone Safari and let's take a tour!

RING-TAILED LEMUR

M Mammal

O Omnivore

Endangered

Y is for YAK

Y is for YAK. Only one hundred in the wild.
I have handlebar horns. and my hair is styled.

I'm the mammal that lives on the highest land.
I can handle the cold, cuz my coat is grand.

Withstanding temperatures at forty below
Fahrenheit and Celsius. That's too cold for snow!

What else can I tell you? There is so much more!
Come to Keystone Safari and let's take a tour!

YAK

M Mammal

H Herbivore

Vulnerable

Z is for ZEBRA

ZEBRA

M Mammal

H Herbivore

*Endangered
(Grevy's Zebra)*

Z is for Zebra. I am black with white stripes..
Plains, Mountain, Grevy are the three different types.

I'm a Grevy Zebra. I'm special, but it's sad.
Some call me Imperial, That's not the part that's bad.

The Grevy are endangered. We're rare you might say.
It's up to you and Keystone to help save the day.

What else can I tell you? There is so much more!
Come to Keystone Safari and let's take a tour!

FUN PAGES
for before or after a visit to
KEYSTONE SAFARI

MY TRIP TO KEYSTONE SAFARI

My Name

A picture of an animal I saw

Date Visited

My favorite animal

ANIMALS I SAW TODAY

- [ ] ....
- [ ] ....
- [ ] ....
- [ ] ....
- [ ] ....
- [ ] ....
- [ ] ....
- [ ] ....
- [ ] ....

NOTES

HERBIVORES

Herbivores are animals that only eat plants.

Penguin	Girrafe	**Cross out the animals that are not herbivores.**
 Hyena	 Zebra	 Mandrill
 Lion	 Camel	 Bear

CARNIVORES

Carnivores are animals that only eat meat.

✗ Cross out the animals that are not carnivores.

Penguin	Girrafe

Hyena	Zebra	Mandrill

Lion	Camel	Bear

OMNIVORES

Omnivores are animals that eat both plants and meat.

| Penguin | Girrafe | ✗ Cross out the animals that are not omnivores. |

| Hyena | Zebra | Mandrill |

| Lion | Camel | Bear |

ANIMAL WORD SEARCH

Find the words listed below and mark them.

A	G	I	R	A	F	F	E	L	R	M	E
N	O	D	U	C	K	P	M	R	E	A	C
T	L	I	F	O	R	E	U	T	C	N	O
G	Y	A	K	D	U	J	W	Q	Y	D	S
O	U	L	B	I	S	H	Y	Z	C	R	H
A	T	I	Z	E	B	R	A	M	L	I	E
T	G	O	O	S	T	R	I	C	H	L	E
P	E	N	G	U	I	N	I	O	N	L	P
Z	N	U	X	L	I	O	N	F	F	O	X

- PENGUIN
- SHEEP
- ZEBRA
- GOAT
- DUCK
- EMU
- FOX
- LION
- YAK
- GIRAFFE
- MANDRILL
- OSTRICH

HELP *Thurman* the SULCATA TORTOISE find the HIBISCUS FLOWER

CAMP

ANIMAL DOT TO DOT

Date: ....

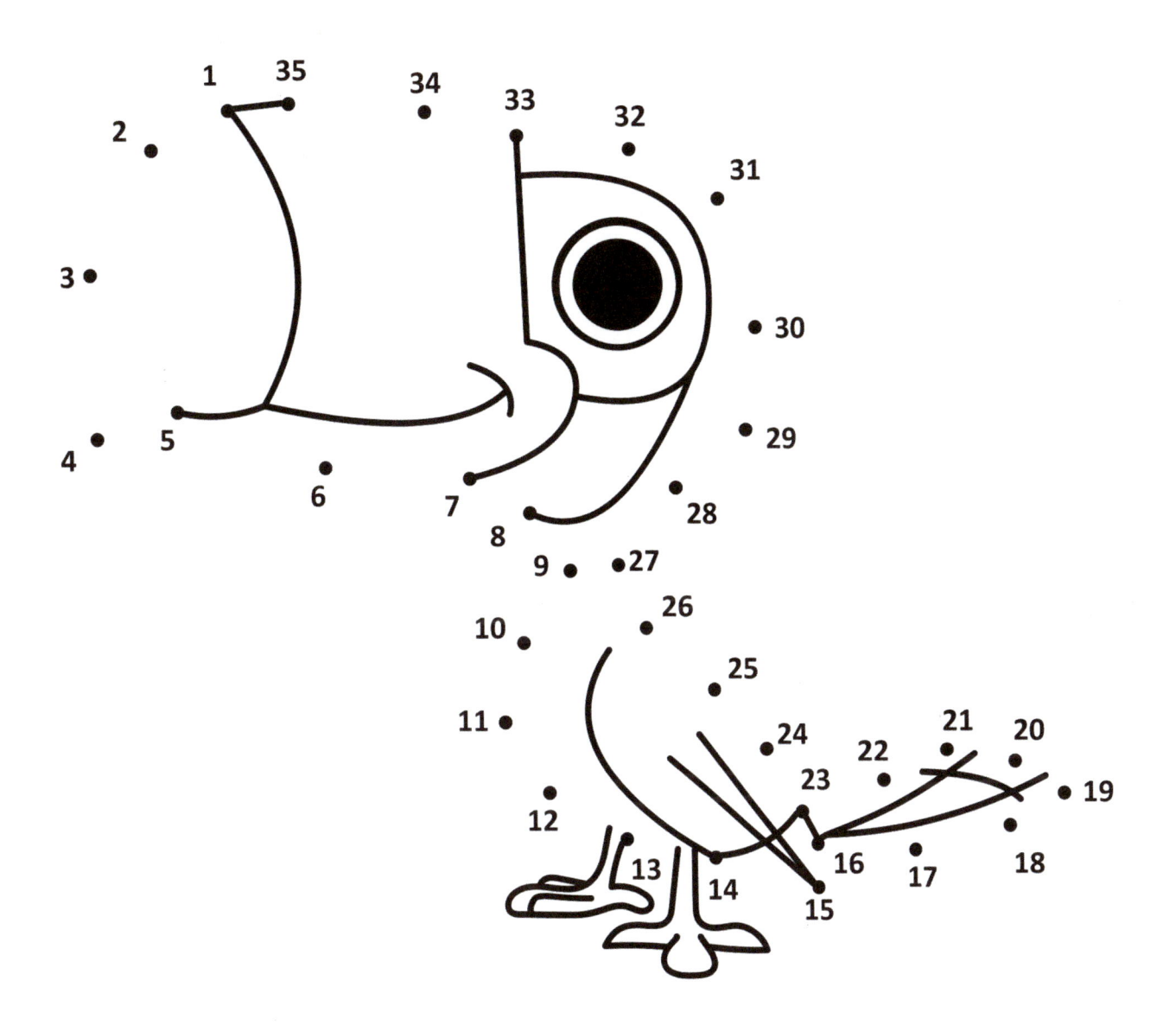

Animal Crossword Puzzle

1. Kookaburra
2. Duck
3. Lion
4. Mandrill
5. Yak
6. Reindeer
7. Giraffe

DESERT

Think of some animals that live in the desert. Draw them or write facts about them on this page.

FOREST

Think of some animals that live in the forest. Draw them or write facts about them on this page.

kookaburra

emu

hyena

ANSWER KEYS

HERBIVORES
Herbivores are animals that only eat plants.

Cross out the animals that are not herbivores.

Penguin ✗	Girrafe	
Hyena ✗	Zebra	Mandrill ✗
Lion ✗	Camel	Bear ✗

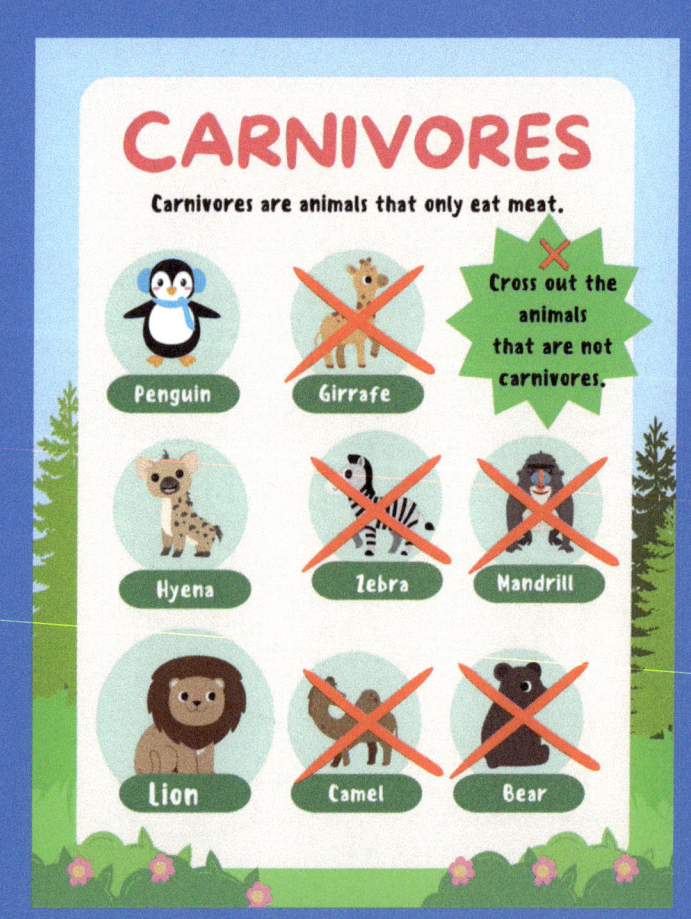

CARNIVORES
Carnivores are animals that only eat meat.

Cross out the animals that are not carnivores.

Penguin	Girrafe ✗	
Hyena	Zebra ✗	Mandrill ✗
Lion	Camel ✗	Bear ✗

OMNIVORES
Omnivores are animals that eat both plants and meat.

Cross out the animals that are not omnivores.

Penguin ✗	Girrafe ✗	
Hyena	Zebra ✗	Mandrill
Lion ✗	Camel ✗	Bear

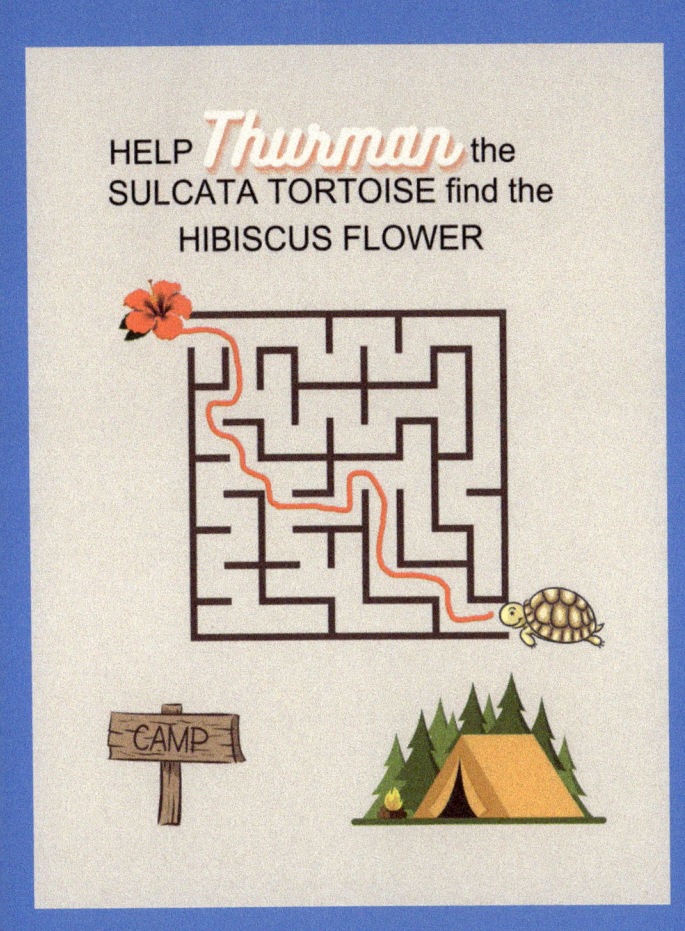

HELP *Thurman* the SULCATA TORTOISE find the HIBISCUS FLOWER

CAMP

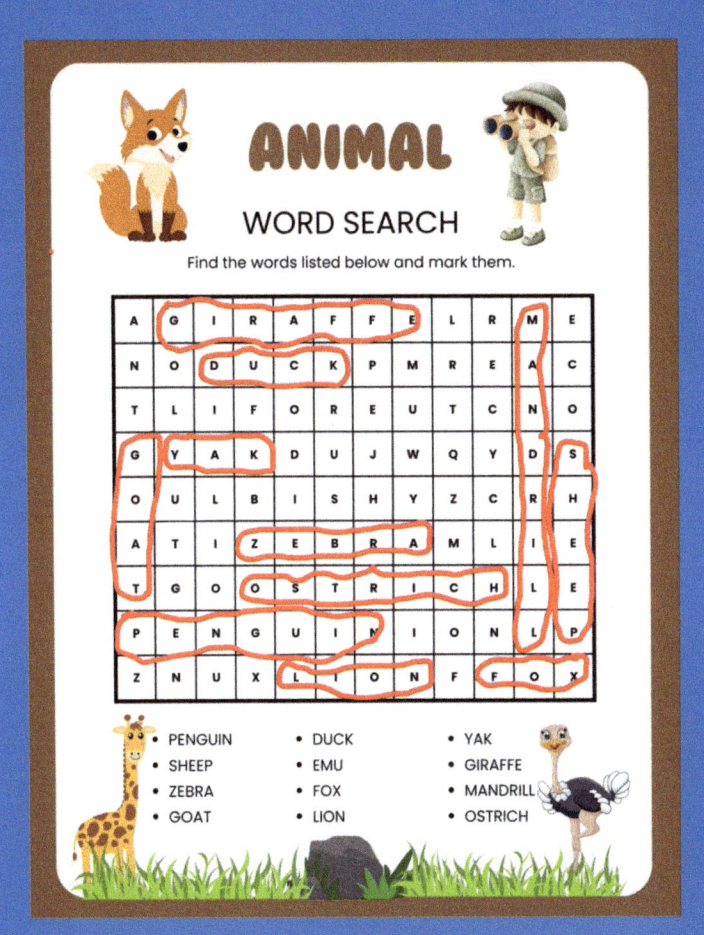

ANIMAL WORD SEARCH
Find the words listed below and mark them.

A	G	I	R	A	F	F	E	L	R	M	E
N	O	D	U	C	K	P	M	R	E	A	C
T	L	I	F	O	R	E	U	T	C	N	O
G	Y	A	K	D	U	J	W	Q	Y	D	S
O	U	L	B	I	S	H	Y	Z	C	R	H
A	T	I	Z	E	B	R	A	M	L	I	E
T	G	O	O	S	T	R	I	C	H	L	E
P	E	N	G	U	I	N	O	N	L	P	
Z	N	U	X	L	I	O	N	F	F	O	X

- PENGUIN
- SHEEP
- ZEBRA
- GOAT
- DUCK
- EMU
- FOX
- LION
- YAK
- GIRAFFE
- MANDRILL
- OSTRICH

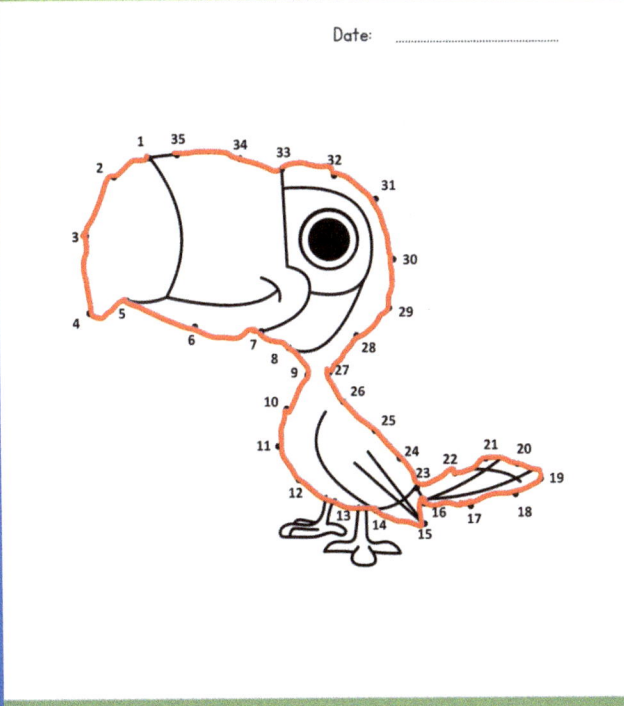

ANIMAL DOT TO DOT
Date: ....

Animal Crossword Puzzle

1. Kookaburra
2. Duck
3. Lion
4. Mandrill
5. Yak
6. Reindeer
7. Giraffe

Milton Keynes UK
Ingram Content Group UK Ltd.
UKHW050752231123
432971UK00009B/81